Acknowledgements

Research on the history of Harringay has been facilitated by the staff at Bruce Castle Museum, Hornsey Historical Society and the various authors on Harringay Online. Several people have helpfully contributed to the descriptions particularly Ian Sygrave of the Ladder Community Safety Partnership, Andy Newman of the Gardens' Residents' Association and Geoff Amabilino of Woodlands Park Residents' Association and not the least our patient wives Marilyn Sparrow and Gill Pengelly. In spite of all this help and support any omissions, errors of fact or opinion are those of the authors.

Generous support has been given to the production of this book by Shefik Mehmet and Rob Chau of the Green Lanes Traders' Association.

Shefik Mehmet
Chair
Harringay Traders' Assoc

Rob Chau
Hon Sec
Harringay Traders' Assoc

Foreword

Harringay has undergone many changes since it developed over 100 years ago. The contents of this book do not set out to be a definitive description of Harringay today but to supplement and extend the description in *How Harringay Happened*, published in 2012. Since then Green Lanes has been transformed by Haringey Council, and the Green Lanes Strategy Group, in two projects funded by the Mayor's Outer London Fund and Transport for London.

This book presents a number of different aspects of Harringay in the form of present day photographs and descriptions of the history and significance of the selection. Harringay is defined by the outline on the 1920s map of the district which shows, by comparison with Haringey's modern street map or an A-Z, that the layout and majority of the streets remain today as they were originally. The name of Harringay in Haringey is also described to help in any confusion between the district and the Borough.

The selected aspects go some way to explore the changes that have occurred and the new developments that have taken place. The area of Harringay includes two parts not dealt with in *How Harringay Happened*, namely the area between West Green Road and St Ann's Road and the area including the Arena Shopping Park and St Anne's Village behind it. The photographs selected are a personal choice by the authors and the associated descriptions provide some background and explain some lesser known aspects of the history, landscape, buildings and streets of Harringay.

We have also included at the end a simple timeline by decade to help describe the continuing development and change of the district.

Contents

Acknowledgements	3
Foreword	4
Locating Harringay	6
The Name of Harringay	8
Listed Buildings	10
Notable Buildings	12
Industrial Buildings	14
The New River	16
Open Spaces	18
St Anne's Village & Finsbury Park Avenue	20
Lords Grove Estate	22
Harringay New Park	24
St Ann's Road	26
Cinemas of Harringay	28
Harringay Grove	30
Arena Shopping Park	32
Harringay Gardens Estate	34
Halls and Community Centres	36
Houses on the Ladder	38
Harringay Passage	40
Railway Fields	42
Flats of Harringay	44
Salisbury Promenade	46
Green Lanes Today	48
A Harringay Timeline	50
About the Authors	52

Locating Harringay

Harringay can be considered as seven distinct areas of urban development numbered in green, straddling the border between Tottenham and Hornsey shown in red on the map of the district in the 1920s.

The area between St Ann's Road and West Green Road [area 1], began to be developed in the 1860s as Lords Grove Estate or Harringay New Park which became a jumble of roads compared to the grid like layout of the rest of Harringay.

The next development [area 2] in the 1880s was the small Finsbury Park Estate to the north of the park itself.

The Harringay Ladder developed between 1880 and 1900 as the Hornsey Station Estate [area 3] and the Harringay Park Estate [area 4] on the west side of Green Lanes.

The estate now known as Harringay Gardens [area 5] was first established as a suburban garden village called Provident Park during the 1890s. The shops along Green Lanes and houses in Salisbury Road [area 6] were developed at about the same time.

The latest development [area 7] of the Arena Shopping Park and St Anne's Village started in the 1990s between Hermitage Road and the railway line and completed the urban development of Harringay.

Harringay, for the purposes of this selection of photographs, is defined by the three wards named as Harringay by Hornsey and Tottenham Councils in the 1920s. Since then many changes have taken place, several as the result of damage during the Second World War. Within this area there are notable histories and features of the landscape, buildings and streets that deserve to be highlighted.

> The detail from Ordnance Survey map supplied by Hornsey Historical Society shows how Harringay looked in the 1920s with the boundaries of the different developments superimposed.

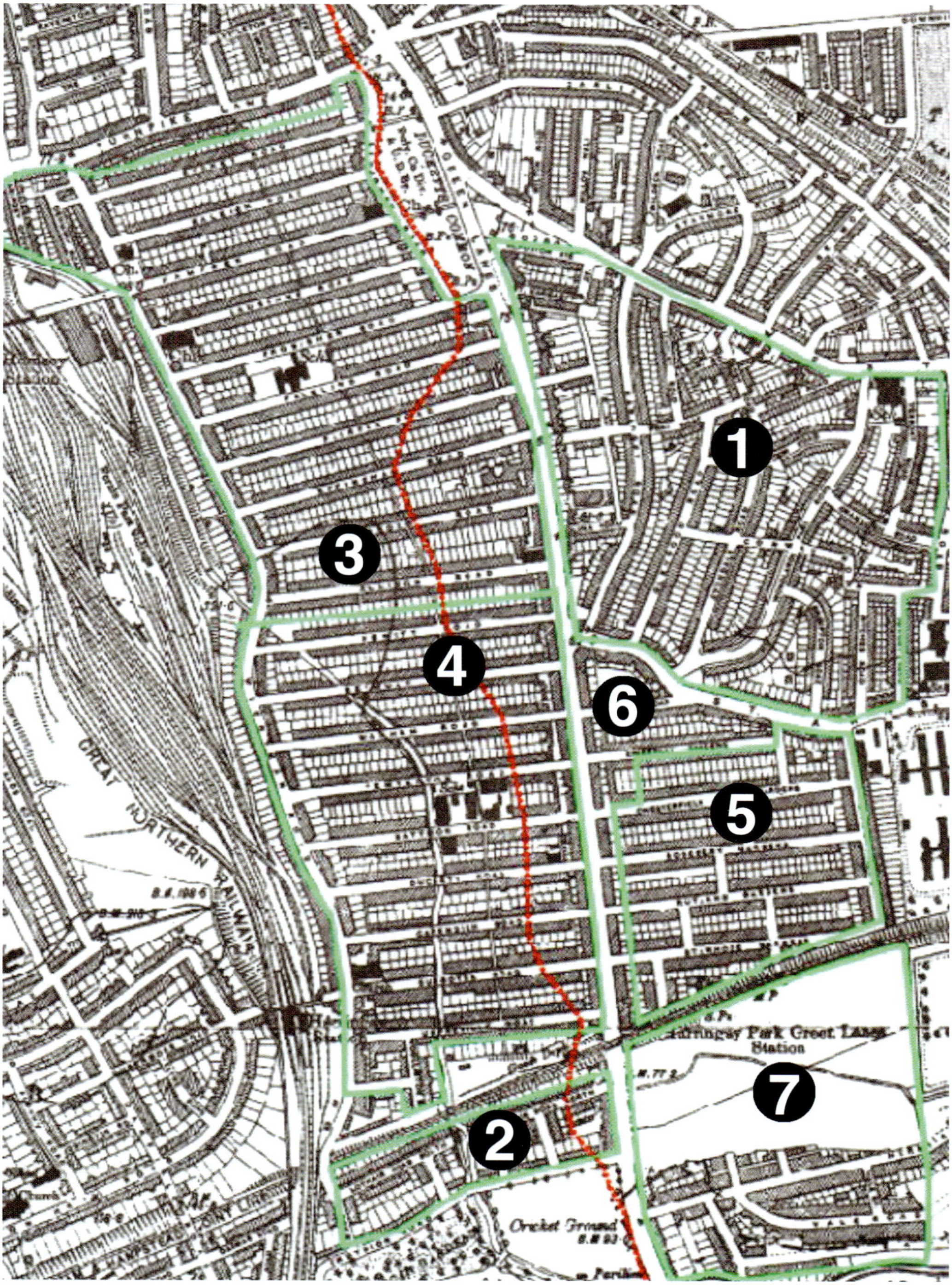
1
2
3
4
5
6
7
School
GREAT NORTHERN RAILWAY
Harringay Park Green Lanes Station
Cricket Ground

The Name of Harringay

The name of the London Borough of Haringey and its relation to the district of Harringay causes much confusion. Fifty years ago no such confusion existed since the London Borough of Haringey had not been formed and the spelling of the name of the district of Harringay was of little consequence.

The London Borough of Haringey was formed in 1965 under the London Local Government Act of 1963 by the amalgamation of the Borough Councils of Hornsey, Tottenham and Wood Green. Representatives of the three Councils formed a joint planning Committee which was required by the Minister for Housing and Local Government to submit a name for the new Borough. After due consideration the representatives proposed to their Councils, each of which agreed, that the name Haringey, being of great antiquity and associated with the central area of the proposed borough, should be adopted.

The names 'Hornsey', 'Haringey', and 'Harringay' all derive from the same Old English word - 'Heringes-hege'. Dr S J Madge (1874-1961), a teacher of English and History at South Harringay School, was the authority who undertook a major study into the origin of the meaning of these names, published in 1936 as the Origin of the Name of Hornsey. The spelling used for the new Borough was the one that Madge had identified for legal and formal use as opposed to the popularly used name for the district - ever since it has caused some confusion in the minds of residents and visitors alike.

Portrait of Dr Sidney Joseph Madge, schoolteacher, antiquary and topographer, in doctoral robes, 1939, courtesy Bruce Castle Museum (ldbcm:2011.577)

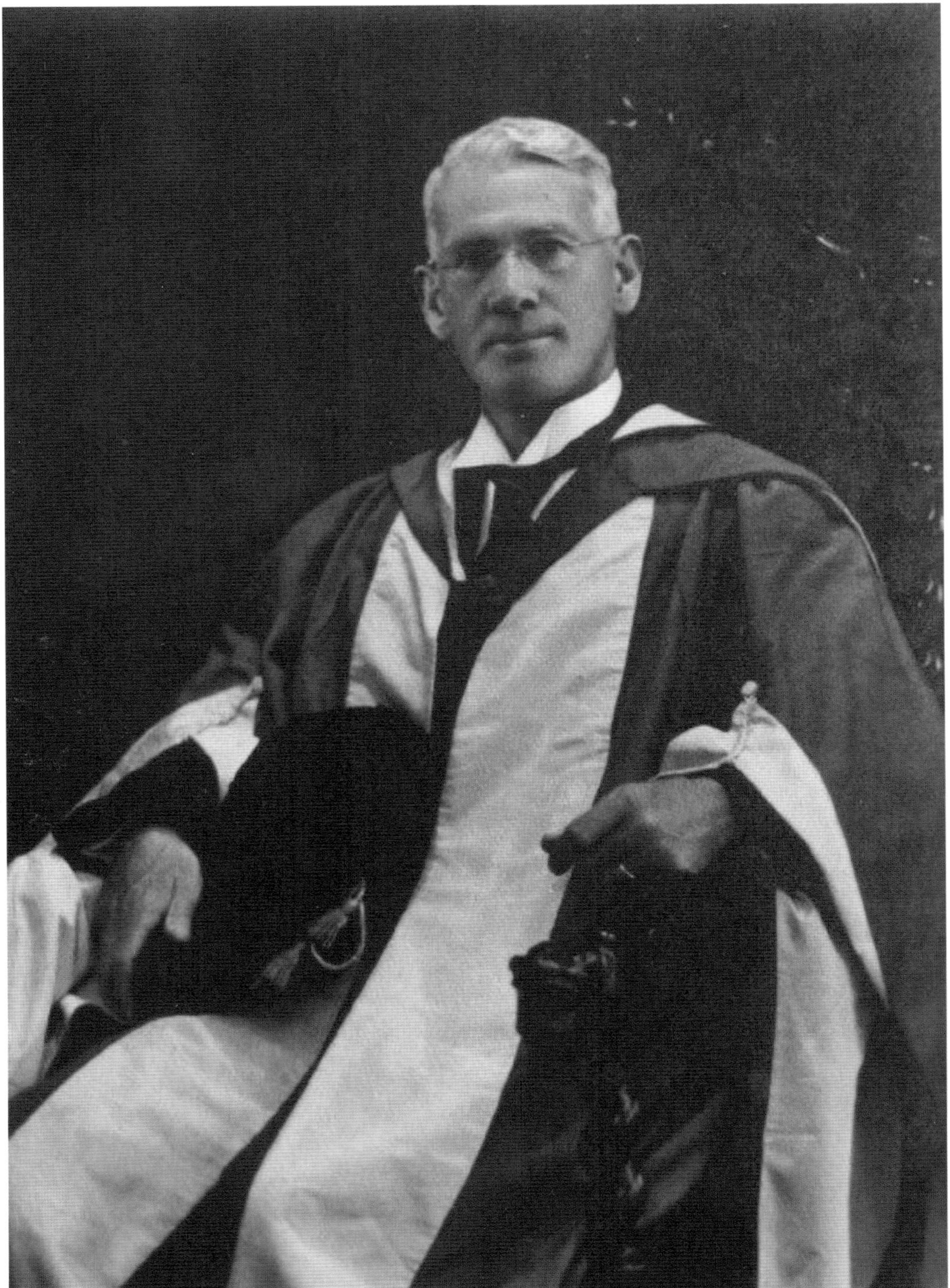

Listed Buildings

Amongst the predominantly residential buildings of Harringay are three buildings that are included in the list maintained as The National Heritage List for England which is the official database that includes all the registered buildings, monuments and parks & gardens of historic or architectural interest.

The three buildings in Harringay are the well known Salisbury Public House on Green Lanes [area 6] that opened in 1899 (listed as Grade II*); the Church of St John the Baptist (Greek Orthodox) formerly the Church of St Peter in Wightman Road [area 3] designed by James Brooks and consecrated in 1887, eventually being completed by 1905 (listed as Grade II*). Next door to the church on the corner of Frobisher Road is the Vicarage of St Peter (listed as Grade II) which forms part of the church group.

The Borough of Haringey maintains a Register of Local Listed Buildings of Merit which includes any building or structure deemed to be of architectural or historic interest which does not qualify for inclusion in the statutory list.

Three features of the New River are included, the tunnel entrances under Wightman Road and at the top of Seymour Road [area 4] and the embankment to the aqueduct in Eade Road [area 7]. Two Public House buildings are locally listed, the Beaconsfield [area 2] and The Queen's Head facing Duckett's Common [area 3], dating from 1794, converted to a furniture shop in 2011. The other locally listed building is the old Conway Road Fire Station built when Conway Road between Avondale Road and Etherley Road [area 1]was developed around 1902. The Tottenham Urban District Council maintained the Fire Station, the first to use petrol driven fire engines, for the Harringay district until 1922 after which it became Firemen's Flats numbers 1 - 4.

> The old Conway Road Fire Station, locally listed, now four flats called Coombes Croft Nos. 1-4.

COOMBES
CROFT
Nos 1-2

Notable Buildings

Two relatively recent buildings in Harringay are notable for their architecture.

St Paul's Church on Wightman Road, between Cavendish and Burgoyne Roads, [area 4] designed by Inskip & Jenkins, opened in 1994 and was described by London Open House as "London's best new church". The new church was built to replace the old church that burnt down in 1983, one hundred years after it opened. A war memorial placed in the church garden in 1920 and maintained by the British Legion as a garden of remembrance after the Second World War, was destroyed by the fire and was not replaced when the new building was opened.

When St Paul's first opened it also had a Mission Hall in Stanhope Gardens [area 5] which survives today as an independent iron church called the Chapel in the Valley.

At the other end of Wightman Road, a new Mosque was built in 1999 on Hampden Road [area 3]; the first custom built mosque in Haringey. The building was designed and built by Crescent Design and Development Ltd., the same company that built the Finsbury Park Mosque. Previously the site had been the home to the community centre of the Islamic Cultural Society. Before that it had been the Hornsey and Wood Green affiliated synagogue that opened in the 1920s, and continued functioning into the 1970s, when its congregation was affiliated with the United Synagogue in Upper Woburn Place.

The newly modified and expanded Mosque on Wightman Road at the corner with Hampden Road.

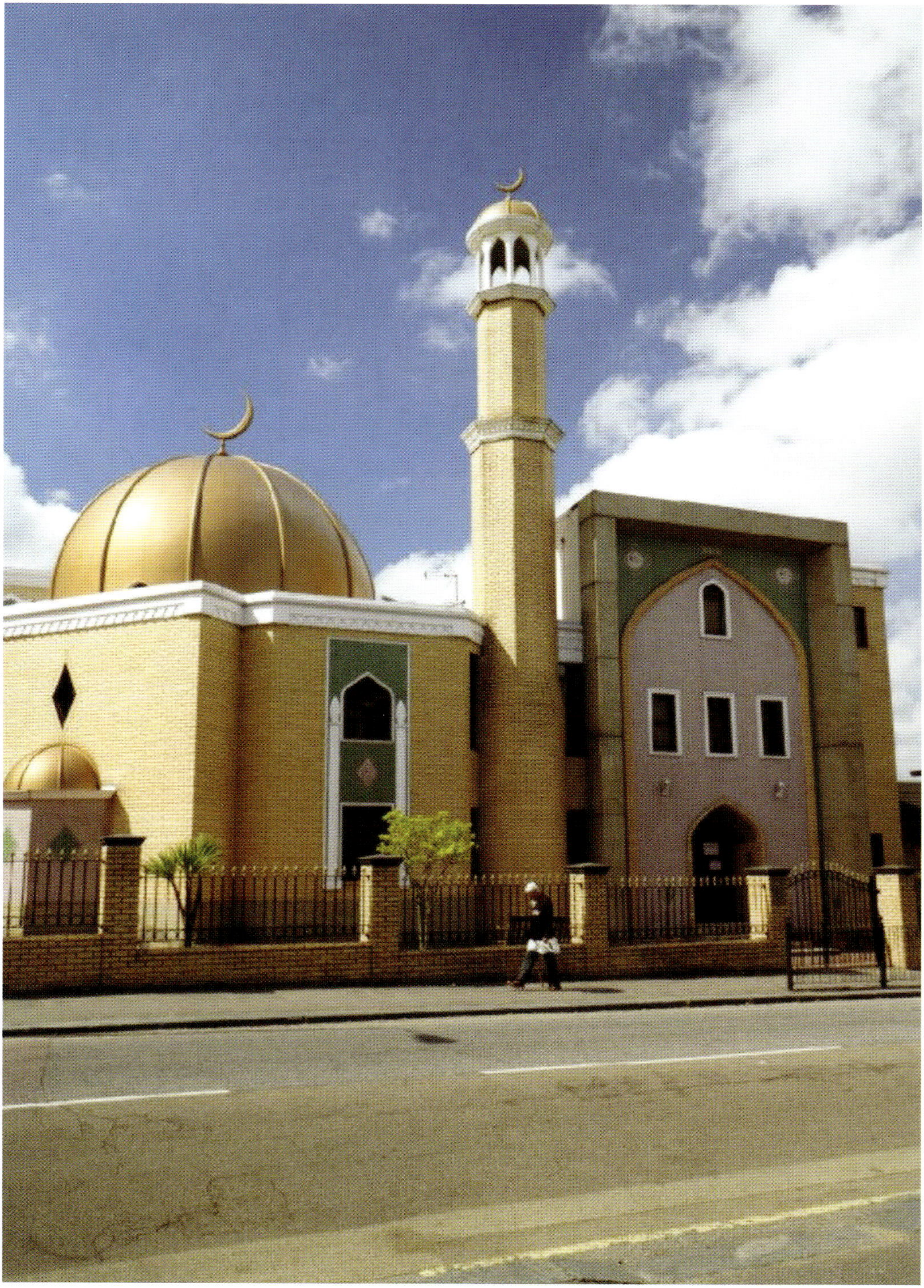

Industrial Buildings

The Willmott Dixon Buildings in Hampden Road [area 3] began in the 1890s when Samuel Willmott opened John Willmott (Hornsey) at 40 Tottenham Lane with a yard in Hampden Road.

In 1969, John Willmott & Sons (Hornsey) Limited became part of a new parent company called John Willmott Construction Limited which was managed by Ian Dixon; the company was renamed in 1987 as Willmott Dixon Ltd. The company grew to be one of the largest privately-owned construction, housing and property development company in the UK., with Inspace amongst the largest social housing contractors.

The Hawes and Curtis outlet on Green Lanes [area 1], was originally Oakwood Laundry in the early 1900s. There are three local authority highways depots; two on Wightman Road [area 4] and one on Conway Road [area 1]; the smallest on Wightman Road, now a motor car workshop, was burned down in 2014 but has since been rebuilt. The other depot on Wightman Road, at the Finsbury Park end [area 4], is now the site of Hornsey Housing Trust's sheltered housing for the Cypriot community. In Conway Road [area 1], Tottenham had a highways depot behind the firemen's flats which has now been turned into private residential housing.

The Hornsey railway depot opposite the Willmott Dixon buildings in Hampden Road has grown enormously since Hornsey station, the first stop out from Kings Cross until Seven Sisters (now Finsbury Park) opened in 1861. Opposite Harringay Green Lanes station, [area 5] originally Harringay Park, Green Lanes, which opened in 1883 was the goods depot which is now Railway Fields. The last station to open in 1885 was Harringay West Station, now simply called Harringay [area 4].

Willmott Dixon's building in Hampden Road which included the company's social housing arm Inspace behind the Mosque.

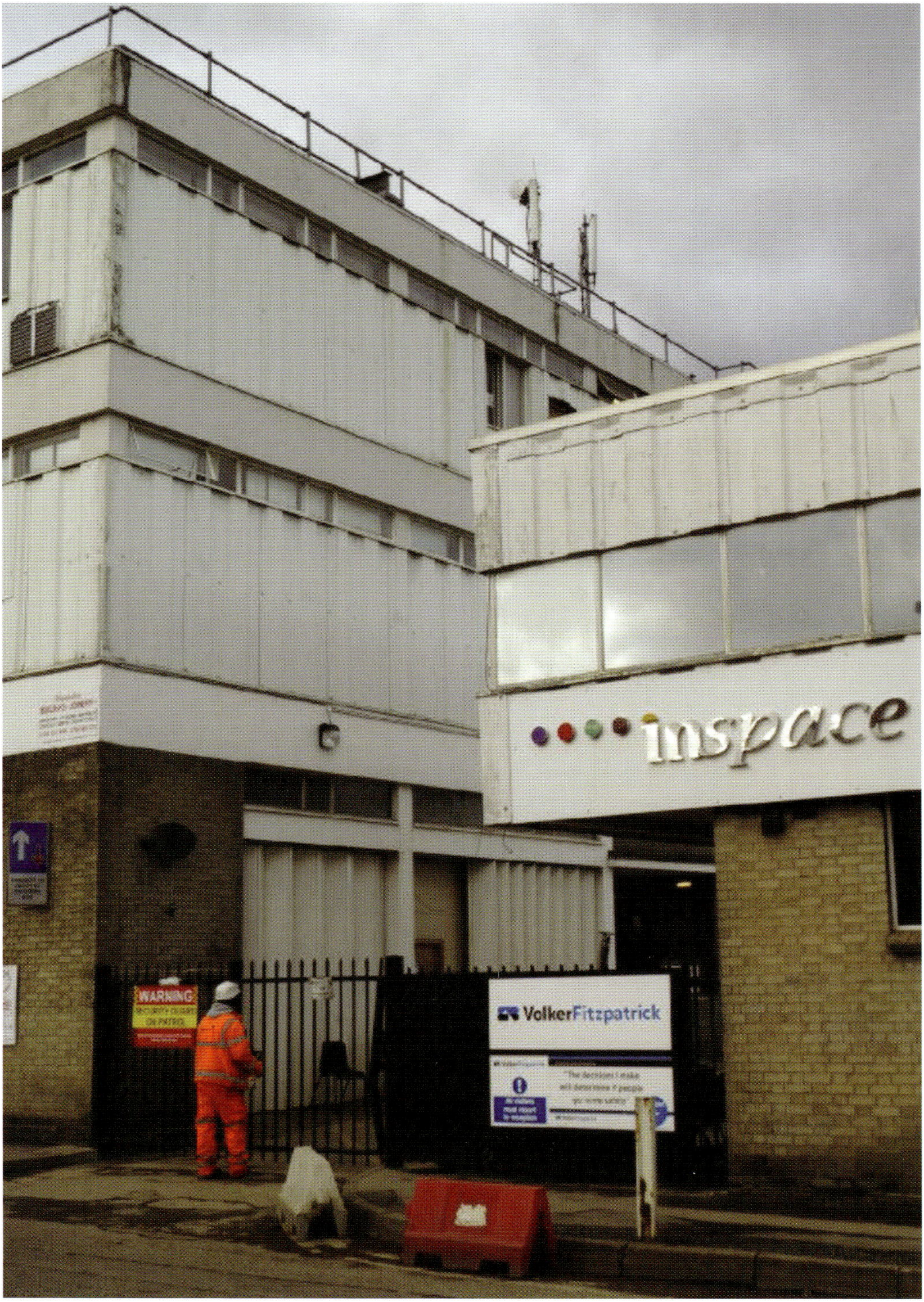
inspace
VolkerFitzpatrick
WARNING

The New River

The New River dating from 1613 is the oldest landscape feature of Harringay. The aqueduct brought fresh spring water all the way from Hertfordshire to Islington for the benefit of Londoners. Originally it wound its way across the parkland of Harringay House in a big loop encircling the house which stood at the top of the hill between Allison and Hewitt Roads.

With the coming of the railway in 1850 and the urban development of the Harringay Ladder in the 1880s the New River had to be straightened out. It now enters a tunnel behind 201 Wightman Road [area 4] and emerges beside number 34 Seymour Road. The aqueduct continues between the houses, parallel to the Harringay Passage, all the way to Finsbury Park.

In 1985 the New River Action Group persuaded Thames Water to create a walking route beside the aqueduct resulting in the path from Hornsey Station between Wightman Road and the railway; a peaceful alternative to walking along Wightman Road. From Finsbury Park it is possible to walk beside the aqueduct across Green Lanes and parallel to Eade Road which marks the southern edge of Harringay.

In the 1860s two streams ran across Harringay from west to east. The Stonebridge brook flowed roughly between Effingham Road and Falkland Road [area 3] to Green Lanes. It then flowed almost parallel to Hanger Lane, now St Ann's Road, underneath Cranleigh Road [area 1]. The Hermitage Brook flowed through the Williamson's Tile works towards the old Hermitage that stood on Hermitage Lane [area 7]. When the Harringay Stadium was built the Hermitage Brook was covered in concrete; so somewhere under the McDonalds restaurant and the Sainsbury's supermarket there may still be traces of the stream.

The New River tunnel mouth under Wightman Road from the bridge on the New River path to Hornsey Station.

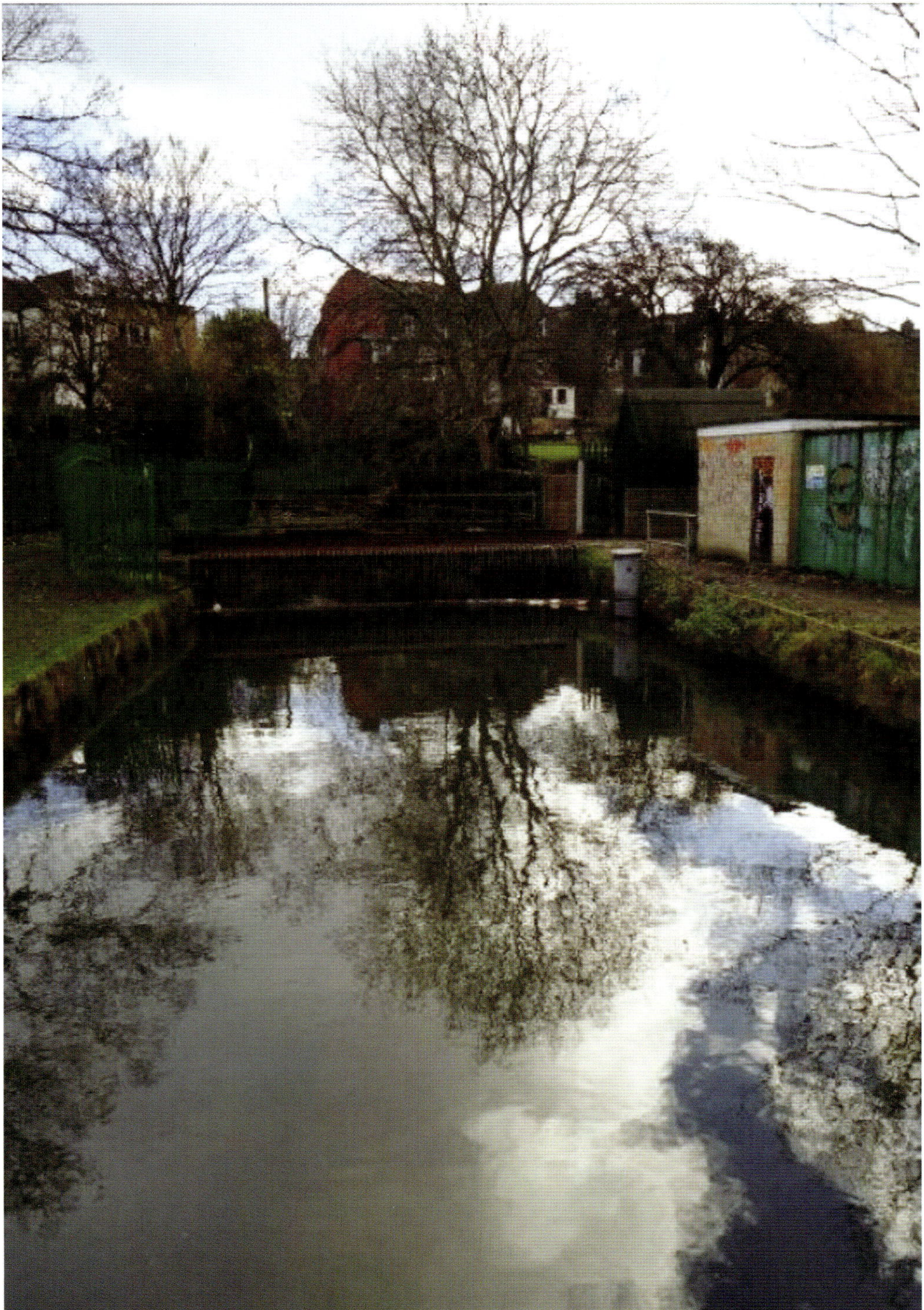

Open Spaces

Harringay developed as a predominately residential area but now includes a variety of open spaces of which Fairland Park, between Fairfax Road and Falkland Road on the 'Ladder' (area 3) is one of the latest.

Pocket Parks have been created, as a result of the re-developments on Lords Grove Estate (area 1), the creation of St Anne's Village (area 7) and the initiative of the Harringay Gardens' Residents' in Doncaster Gardens. (area 5). These open spaces to supplement the much older open spaces created at Railway Fields (area 4) and by the New River.

The park beside Wightman Road was previously known as Log Cabins Park due to the Log Cabin that housed the Hornsey Ridge children's playgroup and after school club. The open space was created as a result of bomb damage in 1944 when the houses on Wightman Road and at the ends of Falkland and Fairfax Roads were damaged and or destroyed.

A small estate of nineteen prefabricated bungalows (pre-fabs) was created on the site and remained there until 1979. The site was taken over as a community amenity and the Log Cabin was built to accommodate the play group and after school club sometime in the early 1980s. The Log Cabin became unsuitable and was demolished in 2007; by 2010 the park had been re-landscaped and a competition amongst local schoolchildren held to find the new name.

> Fairland Park containing a five a side football pitch, a children's playground and landscaped open space on the site of the bomb damage and pre-fabricated bungalow estate

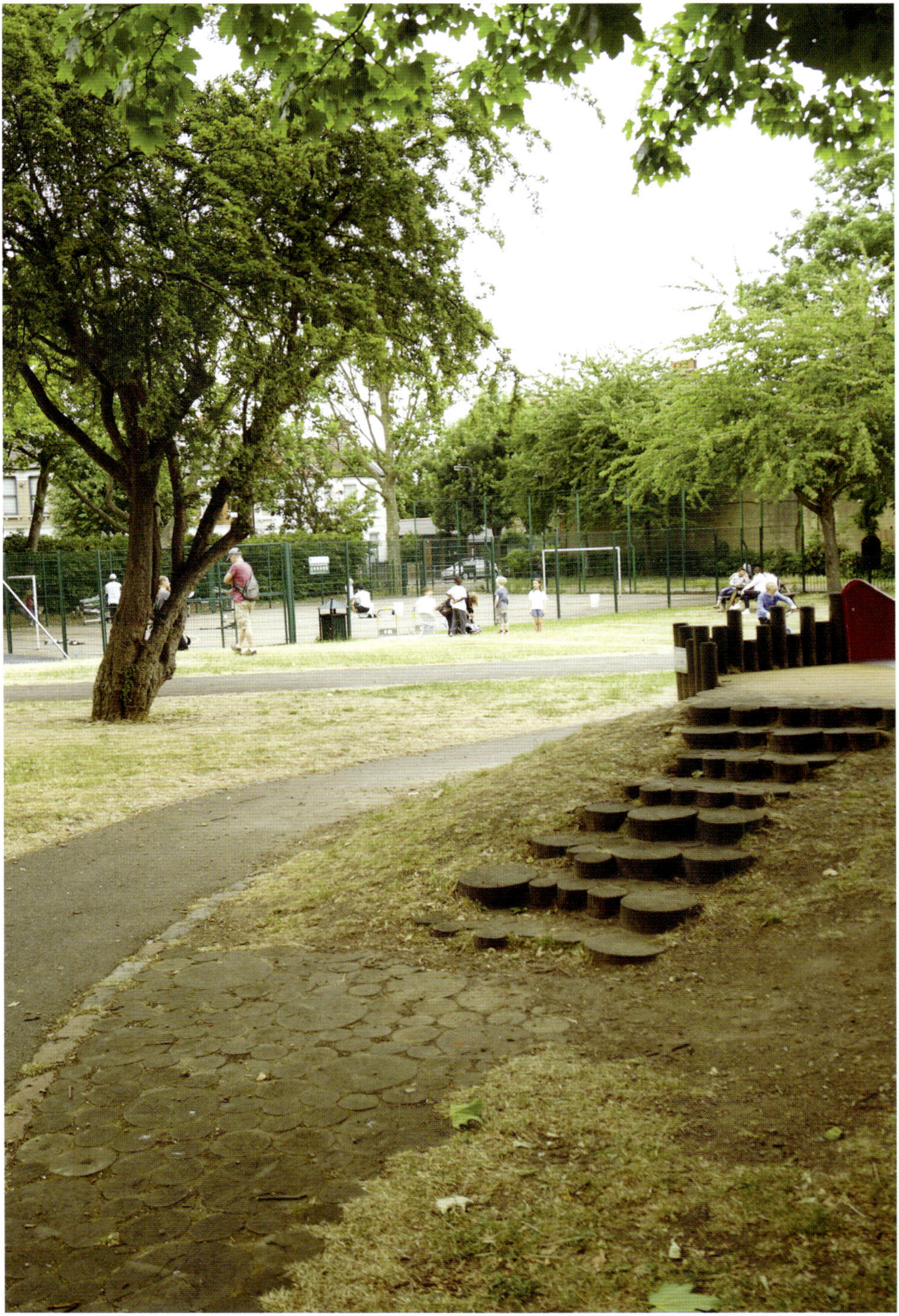

St Anne's Village, Finsbury Park Avenue

Harringay's latest housing development, named by the London & Quadrant Housing Trust as St Anne's Village, is behind the Arena Shopping Park. It stands on a pattern of new roads created as an extension of Finsbury Park Avenue, which was originally a short cul-de-sac off Hermitage Road containing just seven houses which still survive.

Finsbury Park Avenue was laid out across the back of the Harringay Stadium site. The steep escarpment which drops down to the Crusader Industrial estate beside Hermitage Road must have been created when the old Williamson's Tile and brickworks was used to dump spoil from digging the Piccadilly Line tunnels to Finsbury Park wich opened in 1906.

Finsbury Park Avenue now extends from the original cul-de-sac past Surrey Gardens, in a curve behind the Sainsbury supermarket to reach Wiltshire Gardens overlooking the Barking to Gospel Oak railway line. The estate is made up of apartment blocks and houses, with a children's playground almost opposite the end of Surrey Gardens.

The earliest development by McAlpine Homes was in 1991 when plans for 146 one and two bedroom flats were approved. A landscaping proposal by BDG Design of Colchester was approved as part of the first phase of residential development in 1992. Later developments by London & Quadrant Housing Trust extended the estate in 2004. In 2009 the L&Q magazine for residents announced that 'The Better Health, Better Life Campaign' was launched in June on the St Anne's Estate in Haringey.

St Anne's Village behind the Arena Shopping Park, along the extension of Finsbury Park Avenue.

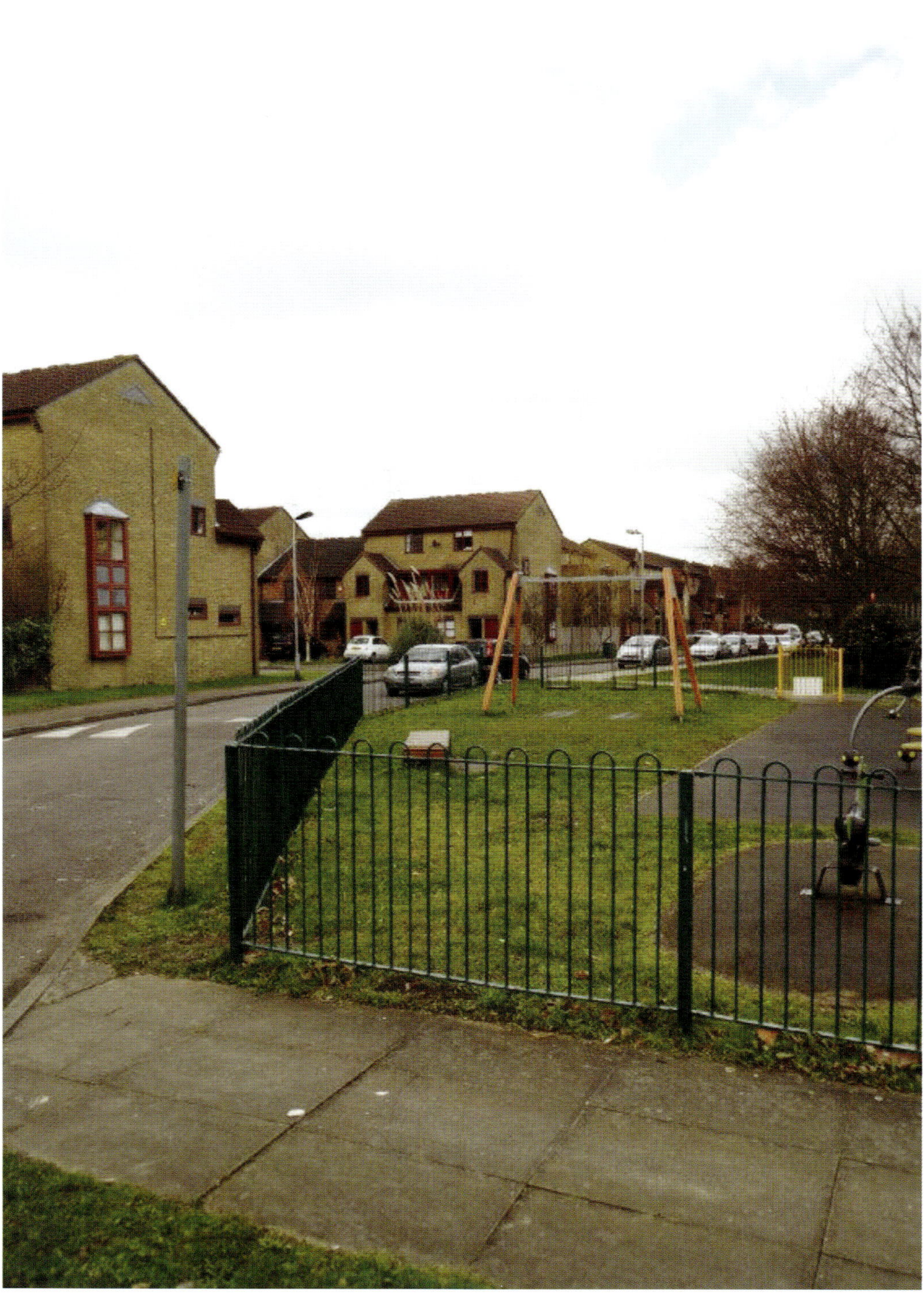

Lords Grove Estate

The very first development of Harringay occurred along the south side of West Green Road in an area known as Lords Grove Estate dating from the 17th century [area 1]. In the 1860s a triangle of Stanley Road, Grove Place and Lansdowne Road (later Culross Road) enclosed Grove Street and Derby Road. By the 1890s Grove Place had become Ely Place, then by 1914 Grove Street had been renamed as Albany Road and Ely Place was called Park Road.

A Primitive Methodist church was built in 1888 at the end of Derby Road on West Green Road. The church was sold in 1969 and used as the Derby Hall Christian Assembly room. Derby Hall played an important role in the redevelopment of the area in the 1970s. The church was demolished and Derby Hall relocated to 425 West Green Road in 1987 when Haringey built the care home called the Red House for 35 people aged over 65 with 17 places reserved for those suffering from dementia. This care home was closed in 2013/14 and Derby Hall, at the time of writing has once again entered into consultations on redevelopment.

Today only Stanley Road remains of the original roads laid out in the 1860s as all the land to Woodlands Park Road is occupied by Albany Close and Culross Close housing estates, taking their names from the early streets, and the Anesty Walk open space.

The entrance to The Red House Care Home 423 West Green Road, now closed to make way for further development of Lords Grove Estate.

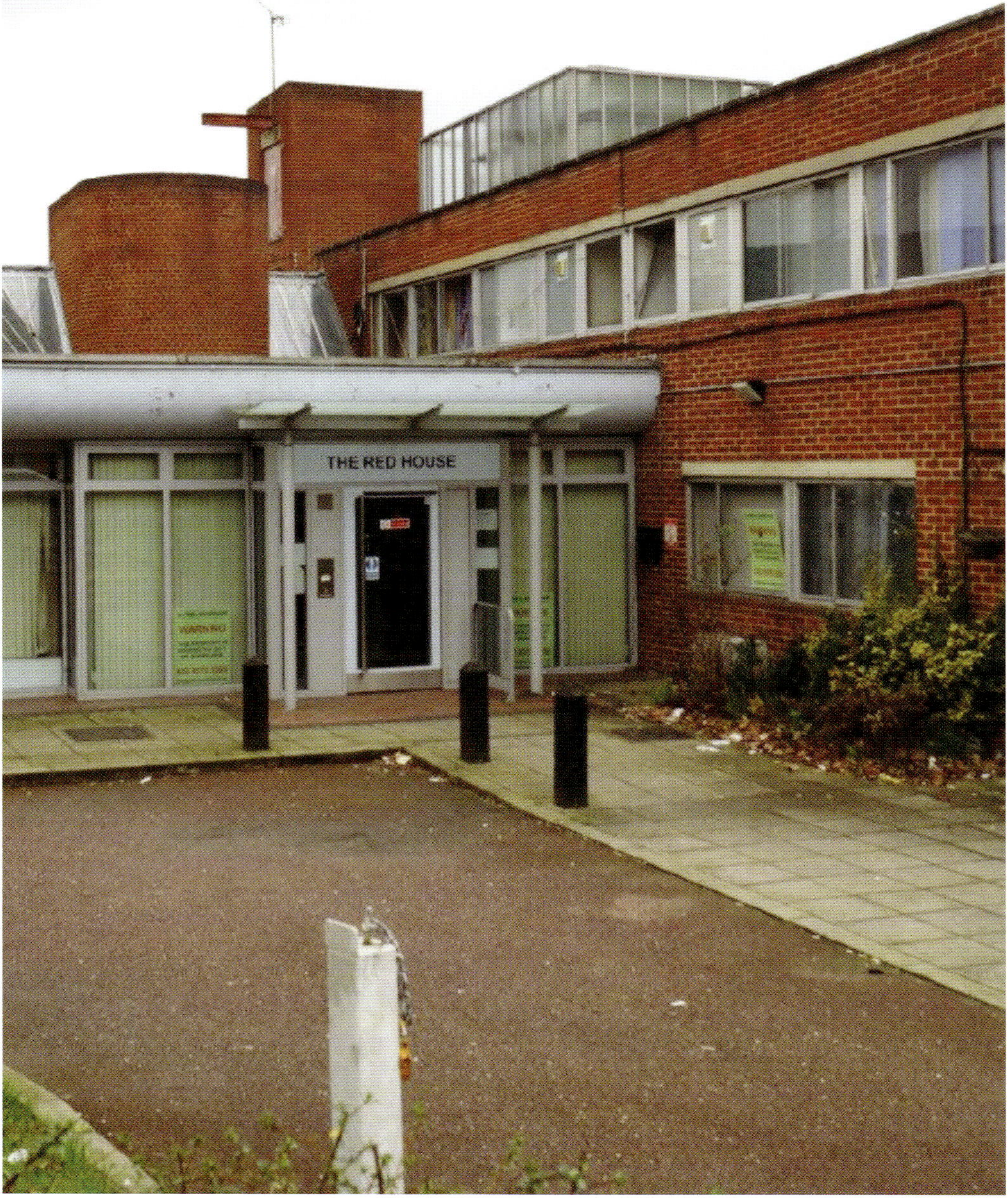
THE RED HOUSE
WARNING

Harringay New Park

In 1880 builders started to develop a new road called Harringay Road on Harringay New Park [area 1]. The first developments were southwards from West Green Road and the road was only fully developed by the end of the century. The name of Harringay New Park does not seem to have lasted, perhaps because of competition and confusion with the British Land Company's Harringay Park Estate [area 3].

Harringay Road is no longer a through road but is interrupted at Park Road which originally ran straight across Harringay Road, but today the continuation is called Hallam Road. This name change and altered road layout is one of many in this section of Harringay.

Colina Road that runs from Green Lanes into Harringay Road was a development by Arthur Vanscolina, a builder of New Southgate, who laid out the new road for a terrace of houses in 1881. These houses, still to be seen, only stood on one side of the road as the back garden of a large villa on Green Lanes occupied the opposite side. When the Piccadilly line was extended in 1932 a ventilating plant was built where the garden used to be and the Oakwood Laundry stood beside it; now the Hawes and Curtis Outlet store.

Further east, the Woodlands Park Estate and Woodlands Park Road take their names from a large house 'The Woodlands' which stood on the northern side of West Green Road, in Linden Road; it was home to the builder Edward Hodson, a younger brother better known William Hodson, of Downhills, who laid out the British Land Company's estates in Harringay. 'The Woodlands' was auctioned off in 1888 and the development of its land gave rise to the most eastern part of Harringay in 1900.

A view towards the Salisbury Public House along Harringay Road on Harringay New Park with the old cinema building on the right.

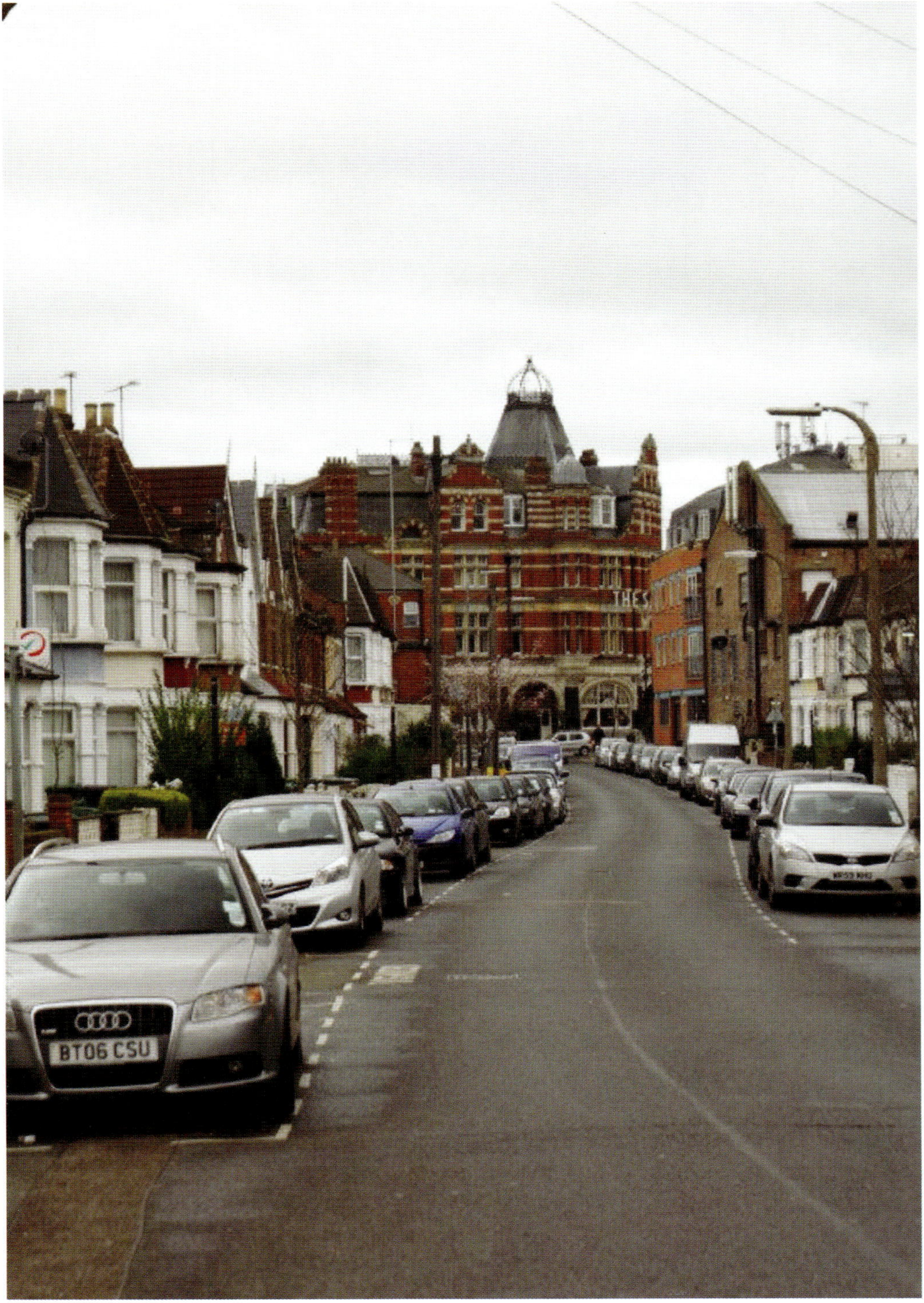
BT06 CSU

St Ann's Road

St Ann's Road is the division between the Harringay New Park [area1] and the Harringay Gardens [area 5]. St Ann's Road was originally called Hanger Green because it led to Hanger Green, a settlement consisting of Hanger Green House, Hanger Green Farm, and St. John's Lodge, that took its name from the lands held by St John of Jerusalem in the 17th century. The name changed from Hanger Green when the new St Ann's church, opposite the end of Hermitage Road was consecrated in 1861.

On the corner of Warwick Gardens, next to the Ambulance station, where Hanger Green House stood, are flats managed by Crabtree Property Management. The Boyd piano works opened a factory here in 1914 but had to move to Clifton Terrace, Finsbury Park, after a flying bomb hit the factory in 1944.

After the war, Ever Ready used the site for their Central Laboratories, where the company's research effort was centred. In 1972 the electrical switchgear firm of Crabtree was acquired by Ever Ready, which then became the subject of a hostile takeover by Hanson Trust in 1981. This may have heralded the closure of the Laboratories, leaving the site vacant for development. By some coincidence Crabtree Property Management, formed in 1984, now manage the small housing estate that opened in 1984.

The Crabtree Property Management flats on the site of the Ever Ready Central Laboratories at the corner of St Ann's Road and Warwick Gardens, where the Boyd Piano Factory stood before the Second World War.

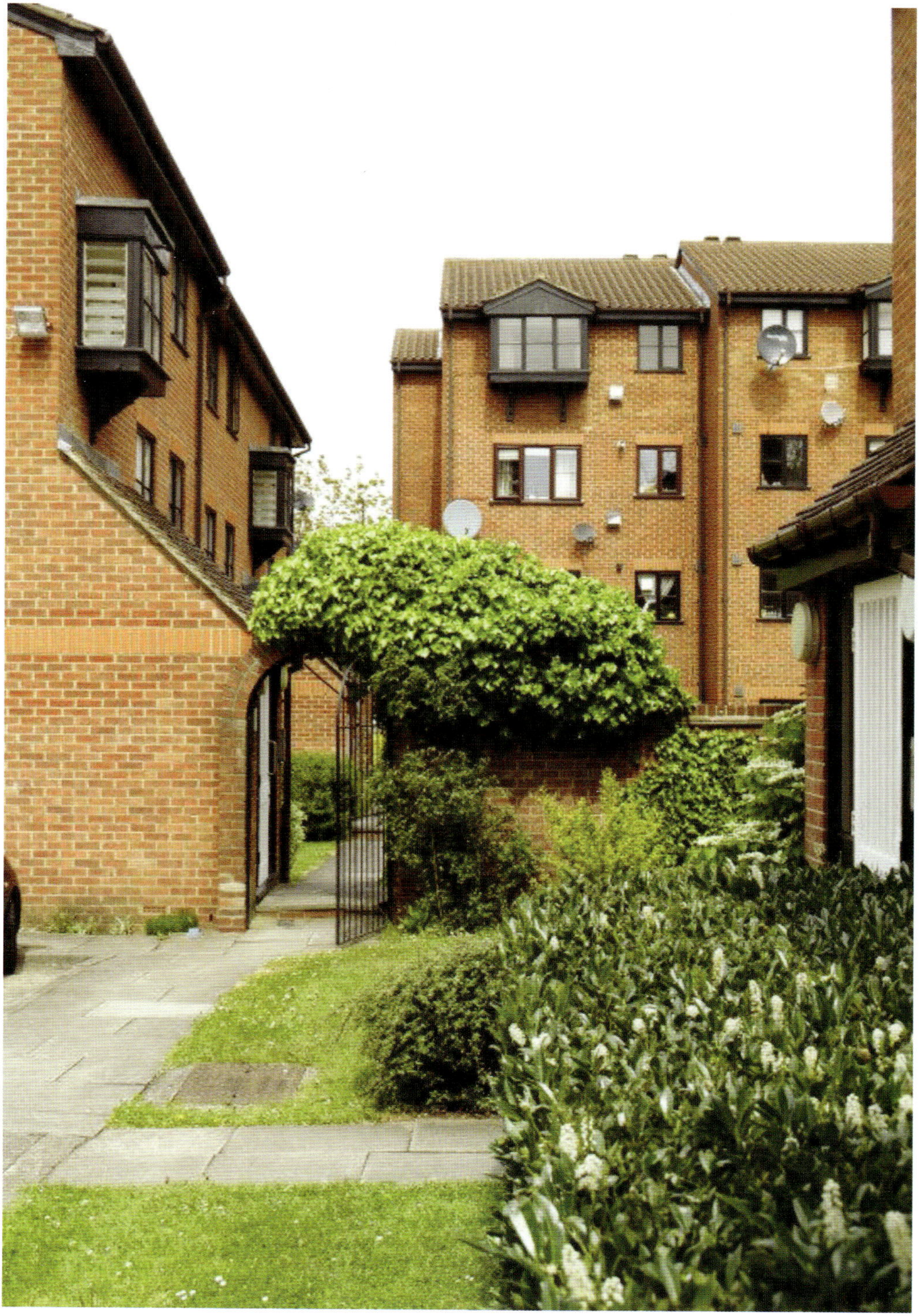

Cinemas of Harringay

On the Salisbury Corner [area 6] is a new block of flats with offices at ground level named the Coliseum after the cinema that was there from 1910 until 1961. The cinema became a bingo hall and then a furniture warehouse and was finally demolished in 1999.

The Premier Electric Theatre opened in 1910 in Frobisher Road, facing Duckett's Common. In 1939 it was renamed the Regal and in 1959 was part of the Essoldo circuit. For a short time in 1963 it was a bingo club before reopening as the Curzon cinema, only to close again in 1989. It then became a laser games venue and was briefly used by the Church of Destiny before being revamped as the New Curzon cinema in 1997, claiming to be the oldest surviving purpose built cinema in London; it is now the Liberty Church.

On the corner of Wightman Road, fronting Turnpike Lane, the Bioscope Picture Palace opened in 1911. It then became the Grand Picture House, Grand Cinema, New Clarence and The Regent Cinema, before closing in 1934, when it was used as a workshop.

Film Locations in Harringay
2010: *Patiala House*: Nikhil Advani Akshay Kumar, Rishi Kapoor: Green Lanes
2009: *London River*: Brenda Blethyn, Sotigui Kouyaté: Harringay Station
2008: *Broken Lines:* Paul Bettany, Olivia Williams, Dan Fredenburgh: Finsbury Park
2006: *Jhoom Barabar Jhoom (Dance Baby Dance)*: Shaad Ali Abhishek Bachchan, Lara Dutta, Bobby Deol, Amitabh Bachchan: Green Lanes, Allison Rd Finsbury Park
2006: *Umut Adası*: Mustafa Kara Halef Tiken, Gürkan Tavukçuoglu: Green Lanes, Turnpike Lane
2005: *Lives of the Saints* :Rankin & Chris Cottam, Marc Warren: Green Lanes, Falkland Road
2003: *Spider*: David Cronenberg, Ralph Fiennes, Miranda Richardson, Gabriel Byrne: The Salisbury Pub (Green Lanes)
1997: *Face*: Antonia Bird, Ray Winston, Phil Davis, Robert Carlyle, Damon Albarn: Harringay Ladder, Wightman Road
1992: *Chaplin:* Richard Attenborough, Robert Downey Jr., Marisa Tomei, Kevin Kline: The Salisbury Pub (Green Lanes)
1980: *The Long Good Friday*: John Mackenzie, Bob Hoskins, Helen Mirren, Pierce Bronsan: The Salisbury Pub (Green Lanes)

The Liberty Church facing Duckett's Common that was the Premier Electric Theatre in 1910.

JESUS
The Prince of Peace
www.libertychurchlondon.net
LIBERTY CHURCH
020 8808 9204

Harringay Grove

Harringay Grove[area 3], like some of the roads on Lords Grove Estate, is one of the few road in Harringay to have completely disappeared. The Turnpike Lane and Wightman Road junction was radically redesigned in the 1970s, sweeping away the old Picture Palace building and creating a new estate of tower blocks. This new estate built over the old Harringay Grove and Denmark Road, which were created by the 1890s as turnings off Turnpike Lane. This corner of Harringay is perhaps often regarded as part of Turnpike Lane , however, in the 1890s when Hornsey first created its North Harringay Ward these roads were definitely part of the new Ward.

The tower blocks have long gone and the present day Denmark Road estate, opposite the end of Sydney Road, has been created using low profile buildings around two cul-de-sacs but the name of Harringay Grove has disappeared.

The road layout of Wightman road has been significantly widened to provide a better access to Hornsey Park Road and all the old houses that fronted onto Turnpike Lane have gone. The Denmark Road estate is now contained behind a wall along Wightman Road, with only one road access beside the Greek Cypriot Women's Organisation building; in that sense it has been largely closed off from the rest of North Harringay.

> The site of Harringay Grove, on what is now the Denmark Road Estate, is a cul-de-sac with only a pedestrian access from Turnpike Lane, which leads up to the New River.

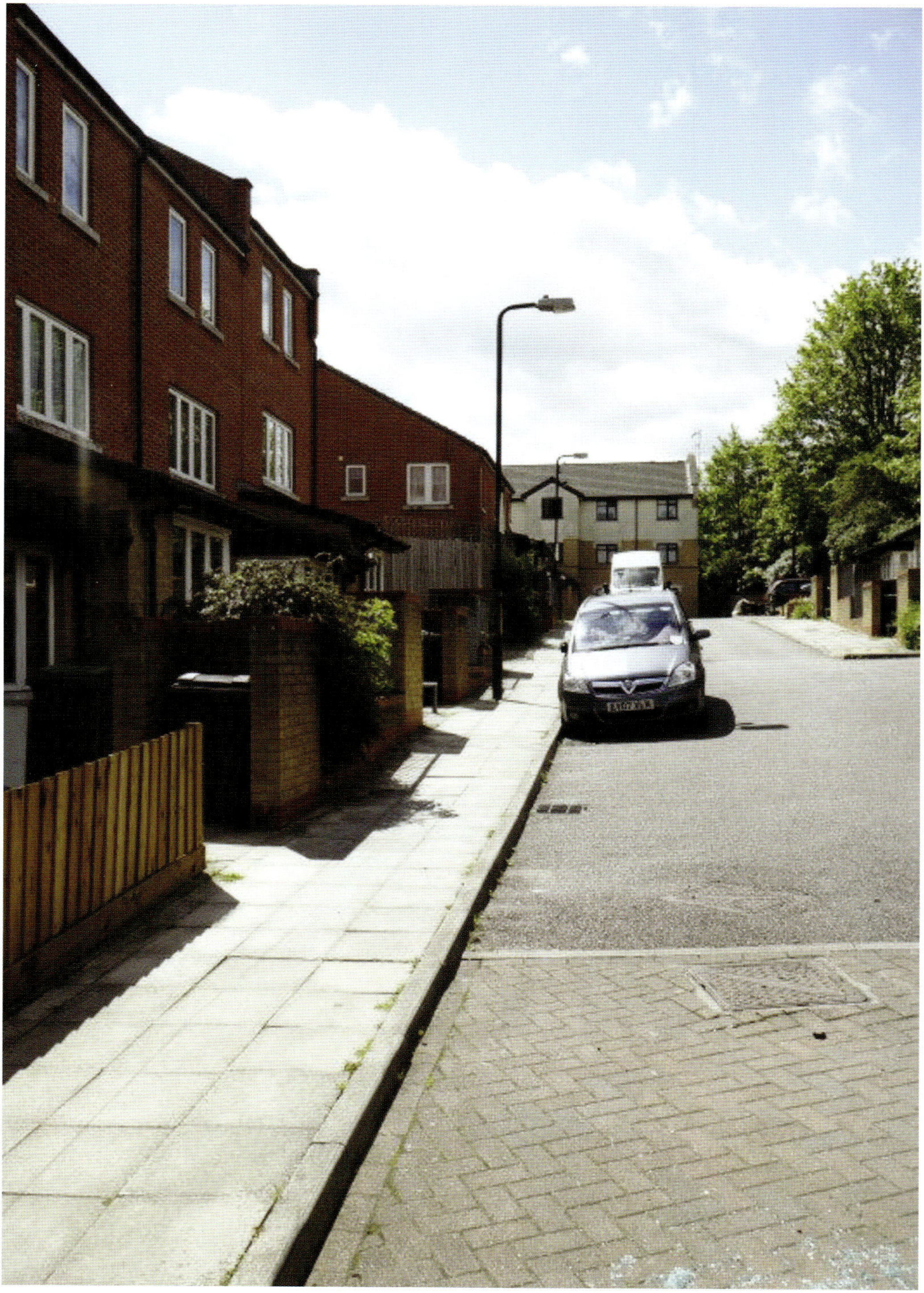

Arena Shopping Park

For many people the dominant feature of Harringay is the Arena Shopping Park [area 7]. This whole area was used in the 19th century as a tile and brickworks operated by W. J. Williamson, who is commemorated in the name of Williamson Road leading into the Shopping Park. The tile and brickworks closed in 1905 and the land was used as a spoil heap for the excavations of the Piccadilly line extension to Finsbury Park which opened in 1906, after which it was a rubbish tip for 20 years.

In 1927, Brigadier-General A.C. Critchley, founder of the Greyhound Racing Association, opened Harringay Stadium as a greyhound race track. The popularity of greyhound racing made Harringay famous. The Stadium also became famous for its automated betting totaliser, which survives today in the Science Museum. In 1936 Critchley opened the Harringay Arena facing Green Lanes, in front of the Stadium, as a boxing and ice hockey venue that could be adapted to host non-sporting events, to rival the Wembly Arena.

The Arena was taken over in 1958 by the Home & Colonial Stores Ltd. as a food storage facility until its demolition in 1978. The Harringay Stadium closed in 1987 and the whole site developed into a warehouse style shopping complex including a Royal Mail sorting office. In 1991 MacDonald's applied for permission to open a restaurant beside the station and in 1992/3 Sainsbury's applied to open a store. The present day Arena Shopping Park, developed by Wildmoor Properties, began in 2000 with what is now Homebase, and incorporated the Royal Mail sorting office. Wildmoor also agreed to the building of 30 flats.

The Arena Shopping Park on Green Lanes where the 1930s Harringay Arena stood.

ARENA
SHOPPING PARK

- Sainsbury's
- HOMEBASE Design Centre
- next
- SPORTS DIRECT.COM 24HR DELIVERY
- The Carphone Warehouse
- SUBWAY
- Dreams
- Poundland
- Argos
- T·K·maxx
- Fitness First
- COSTA

Harringay Gardens Estate

The Harringay Gardens Estate [area 5] is not to be confused with the road named Harringay Gardens [area 1] which is a cul-de-sac off Green Lanes opposite the end of Fairfax Road. The Harringay Gardens Estate started in 1890 as Provident Park and was meant to be a garden suburb for the working classes.

The Provident Association of London Limited offered a life assurance scheme whereby families of weekly wage earners, with little or no capital, could purchase a house after five years of paying into the scheme. In Tottenham the company built one of its few estates to the designs of their own architect and surveyor, Thomas E. Haines. Hence the majority of the houses in the Harringay Gardens estate appear very similar.

This nationwide scheme appeared attractive, but if regular payments were not maintained for whatever reason, or if the wage earner wished to withdraw from the scheme due to unemployment, they discovered it was not possible to redeem the investment. Many people began to feel they had been misled into paying money into the scheme from which they were unable get any benefit. By the 1900s this early example of mis-selling went to court and the Provident Association was reprimanded.

The estate did not turn out as a garden suburb, but tucked away in Doncaster Gardens, off Stanhope Gardens, is a pocket park created in what used to be a back entrance to the site of the Harringay Stadium, and later the Sainsbury's supermarket. This entrance was closed off and opened by the Gardens Residents' Association as The Gardens' Community Garden in 2002 and was awarded a Green Pennant or Community Green Flag, in 2006, and has been a winner ever since. The garden, designed by Andy Newman of the Residents' Association, is frequently used for community events including out door films shows.

Doncaster Gardens, the prize winning Community Garden maintained by the Garden Residents' Association.

The Gardens

GRA

Halls and Community Centres

When the Harringay area was built, churches and pubs provided spaces for community use, for example St Pauls' used number 56 Burgoyne Road as a Parish hall before the First World War [area 4]. The Beaconsfield was a meeting place for the Primrose League [area 2]. Other community halls were also created. The Harringay & Green Lanes Constitutional Hall and Club, a Conservative Party Institution, was built at 632 Green Lanes [area 3]. Nearby at 611 Green Lanes was the Harringay Liberal Social Institution. The Langham Club and Institute, started as The Hornsey Social Club, in Turnpike Lane, affiliated to the Working Men's Club and Institute Union, and relocated to Green Lanes in 1915 [area 1].

In 1996 the Kurdistan Workers Association took over the old Fairfax Hall, 11 Portland Gardens [area 5]. In 2006 a memorial garden was created behind the Hall to the memory of Ugur Kaymaz who was killed on 21 November 2004 in Kiziltepe district of Mardin, Police pending trial were acquitted but the Court ruled that Turkey had violated Ugur's right to life.

In 1996 the Kurdistan Worker's Association took over the old Fairfax Hall, 11 Portland Gardens [area 5], which was variously used as a venue for dancing, a clubhouse for the Finsbury Park Cycling club, a centre for civil defence and a meeting place for the Socialist Party of Great Britain before becoming a factory/warehouse in 1949. In 2006 a memorial garden was created behind the Hall to the memory of Ugur Kaymaz who was killed by police on 21 November 2004 in Kiziltepe district of Mardin. The Court eventually ruled that Turkey had violated Ugur's right to life. Andy Newman designed and built the memorial garden with labour provided by the probation service.

Memorial Garden created by the Kurdistan Worker's Association behind the Fairfax Hall in Portland Gardens.

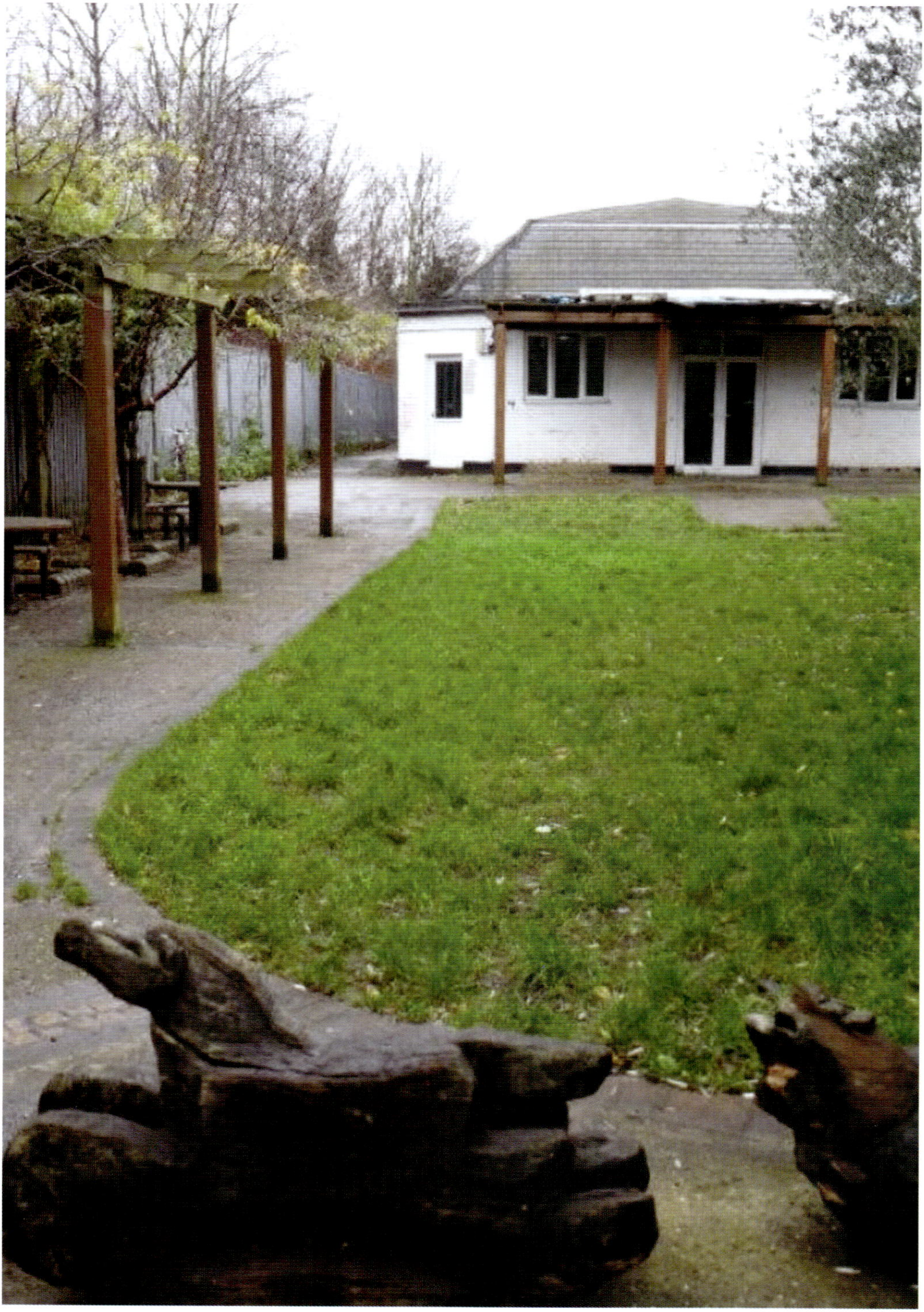

Houses on the Ladder

It is not clear when the roads between Wightman Road and Green Lanes became known as the 'Ladder', but the reason is that on the map they look like rungs of a ladder.

The Golden Jubilee edition of the Hornsey Journal in 1929 recalled the development as a great transformation; Harringay was the scene of the first big building operations in Hornsey involving mass production methods.

The developments by speculative builders started in the 1880s from Turnpike Lane and worked south on the Hornsey Station Estate (North Harringay), and from the other end working north on the Harringay Park Estate (South Harringay), so that all the 'Ladder' streets were complete by about 1900. Wightman Road was built at this time, probably, initially as an access road to the building operations on the side streets.

The entry for Harringay in Pevsner's Buildings of England; London 4 North is rather dismissive: "Its only notable buildings are the churches and schools built to serve the 'ladder' of streets north of Finsbury Park, laid out unimaginatively by the British Land Company in 1880-1 over the site of Harringay House and its grounds."

One of the distinctive characteristics of the housing on the 'Ladder' is the diversity of styles and appearances of the houses. Number 45 Warham Road is the most unusual house squeezed into a triangular site beside the New River as an after-thought by Mr Fox who added this house to the two he built next door in 1893. The houses from numbers 51 – 77 are more typical, which is hardly surprising as they were built by the Davis brothers John and William Henry, the largest developer of the 'Ladder'.

Number 45 Warham Road, once described as the 'back to front' house. The porch is very similar to the ones on numbers 47 and 49 also built by Mr Fox.

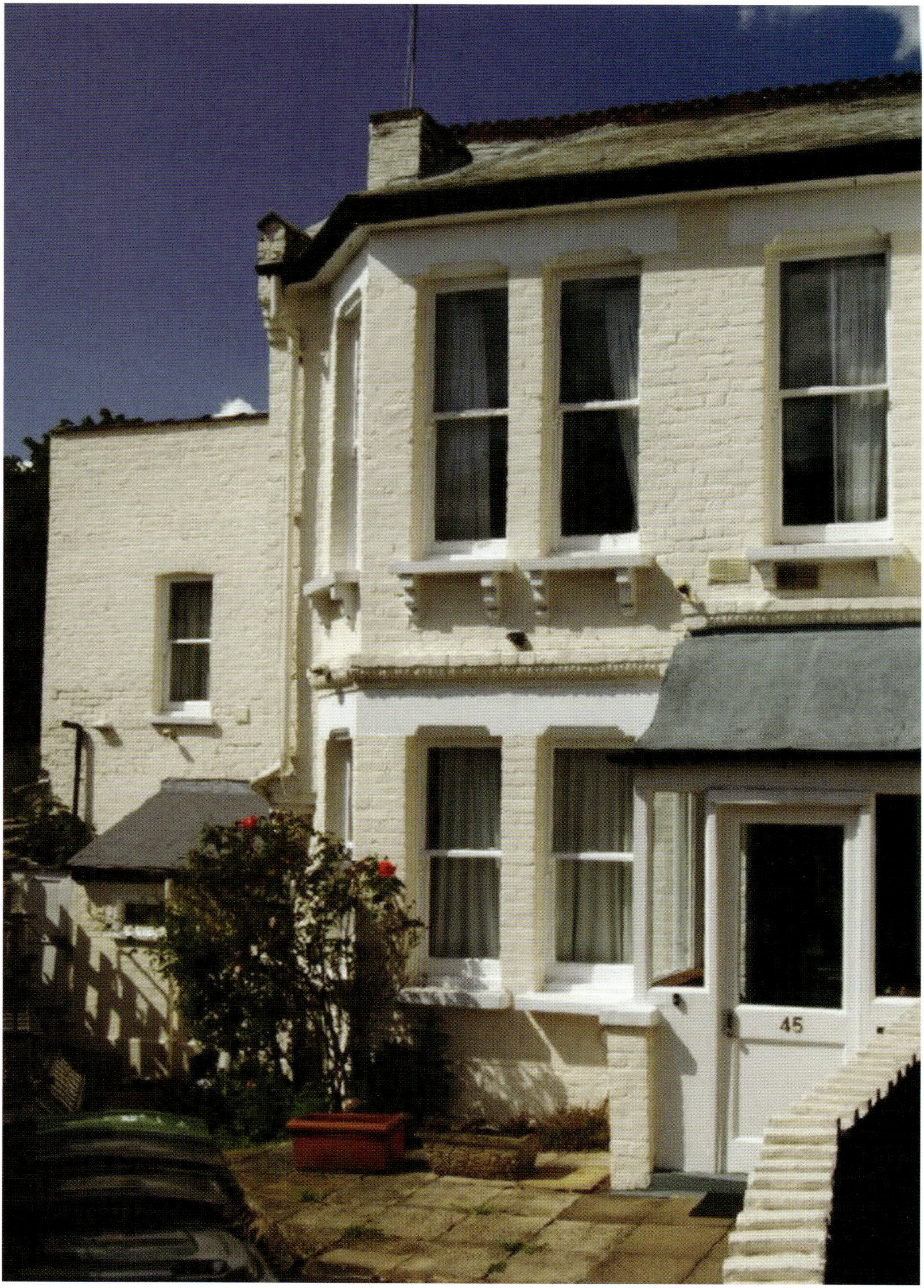
45

The Harringay Passage

There are two distinctive features of the 'Ladder' other than the houses, both of which are monuments to significant civil engineering achievements of their times.

The New River opened in 1613 to bring fresh drinking water from Hertfordshire to Islington, is neither a river nor is it new. It now provides an off-road walking route in North Harringay from the Mosque to Allison Road.

The other feature is Harringay Passage. In 1869 the civil engineer Baldwin Latham proposed a system of sewers to drain the whole parish of Hornsey. In the 1870s, the Hornsey Outfall Sewer was laid across the parkland of the old Harringay House to link up with London's Northern High Level Sewer, south of Finsbury Park. As the 'Ladder' streets were laid out, houses could not be built above the outfall sewer. Thus a gap which is now the Harringay Passage appeared between the houses as they were built.

The Passage was paved in York stone in stages between 1887 and 1890. By the early 20th century the sewer had to be upgraded and the Passage was progressively excavated to provide improvements. A surge tower was built in the old goods depot (now Railway Fields) behind Umfreville Road in order to prevent overflows flooding properties beside the Passage.

A few of the original features of the passage can still be seen such as some sections of York stone paving, the moulded drainage gulleys and drain covers, and the cast iron stench pipes. Some of the old, pre-1965, Haringey Passage signs, high up on the walls, contrast with the newer signs spelling Harringay Passage.

Beside the North Harringay School the brick wall is heavily inscribed with graffiti dating back to the nineteenth century when the school was first built by the Hornsey School Board.

Graffiti from the late 19th century carved into the brickwork of the Harringay Passage wall beside North Harringay School.

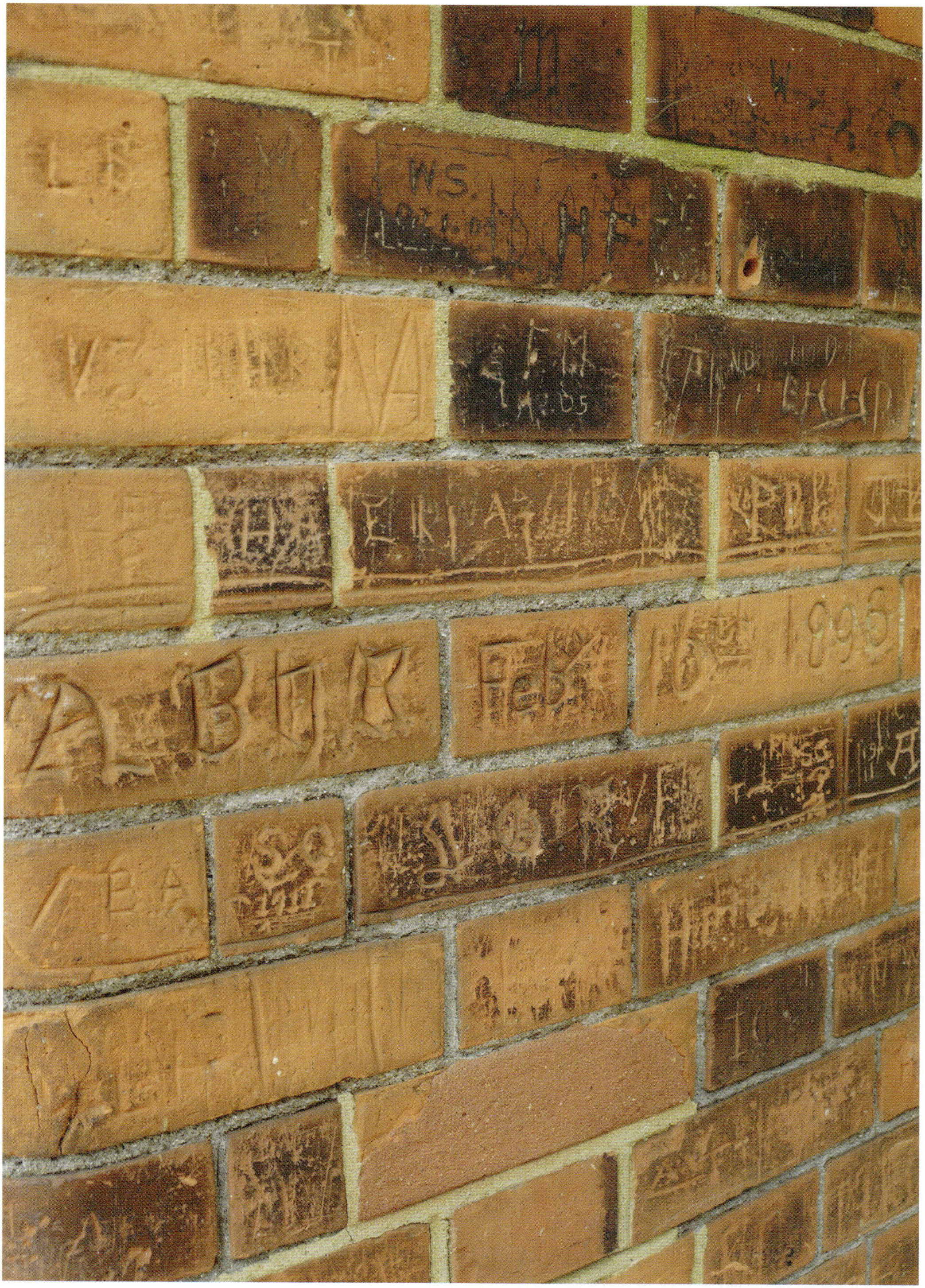

Railway Fields

The gates to Railway Fields, on the opposite side of the Green Lanes to the station entrance [area 4], stand out as a fine example of artistic embellishment to the street scene.

Apart from the decoration on the houses, some of which is truly outstanding such as the swags on the bays of houses in Cavendish Road, or the porches to houses in Pemberton Road [area 4], there is not a great deal of street art in Harringay. Outside number 7 Willoughby Road [area 3] is a modernist sculpture entitled 'Monument to Engineering Works'. A plaque explaining the Monument has a signature which is illegible, and there is no date given. Why it was installed remains unknown.

Railway Fields was originally the goods depot of the Harringay Park, Green Lanes, Station opened in 1883. The station name lasted until 1951 when it was renamed, to just plain Harringay Park; seven years later it became Harringay Stadium. After the stadium closed the name of the station changed in 1990 to Harringay East, becoming Harringay Green Lanes in 1991.

The old goods depot opposite the station entrances closed in 1967, eventually becoming, in 1985, Railway Fields, Haringey's first nature reserve and teaching centre. The gates were designed by Heather Burrell and made in the artist's own studio in Deptford and installed at Railway Fields in 2002. Behind the magnificent iron gates lies one of Harringay's most hidden and wonderful treasures.

The decorative iron gates, by Heather Burrell, to Railway Fields on Green Lanes, opposite Harringay Green Lanes Station.

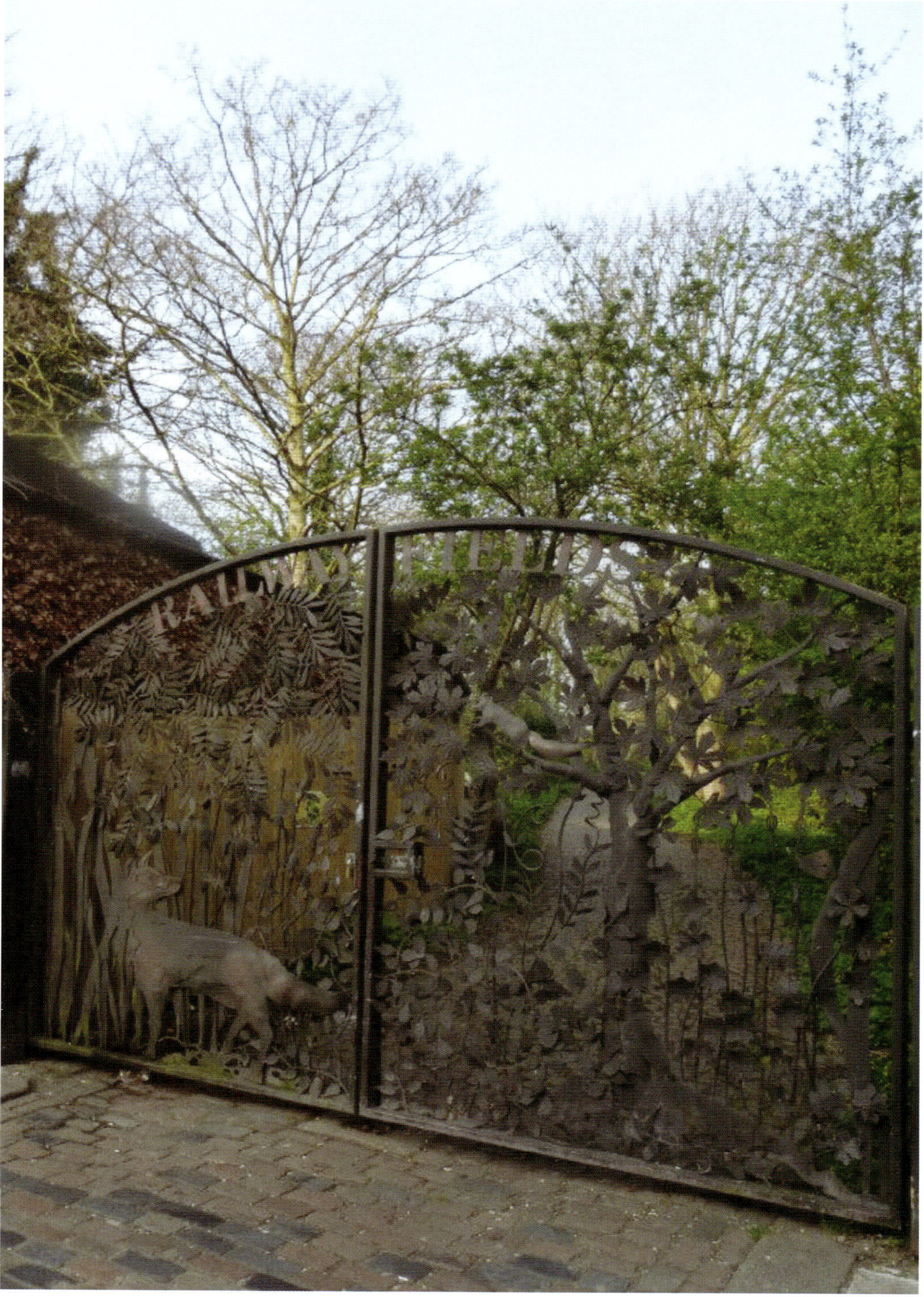

Flats of Harringay

Most of the dwellings in Harringay are in the form of houses built in the late 19th century, with later additions in the form of flats. The first block of flats to be built in 1898 were those of the Station Mansions in Wightman Road. [area 3] These were followed in 1900 by the smallest block of four flats in Harringay at 71 Kimberley Gardens [area 5]. The two large blocks of flats on St Ann's Road called Salisbury Mansions opened in 1903.

Mountview Court on Green Lanes [area 1] is a distinctive Art Deco design which opened in 1937. This private development was taken over by Tottenham Council in the 1960s as part of the council strategy of improvements. The owners, faced with the prospect of a compulsory purchase order, decided to offer the council the chance to buy the flats at an agreed price to save the costs of the legal process. The flats are now managed by Homes for Haringey.

The Second World War brought with it considerable damage to Harringay as a result of air raids. Several council blocks of flats appeared after the war on sites previously occupied by private houses in Wightman Road [area 3 & 4], Fairfax Road, Sydney Road, [area 3] and Warwick Gardens [area 5]. Later council redevelopments emerged at Culross and Albany Courts just off West Green Road [area 1].

In the last few decades several new blocks of flats have appeared as a result of private re-development of various sites; the replacement of St Paul's Church included a scheme of flats [area 4]; the development of the Arena Shopping Park involved new blocks of flats [area 7]. One of the more distinctive blocks, Paragon Court, is on Wightman Road almost opposite Station Mansions [area 3].

Mountview Court flats on Green Lanes, opposite Duckett's Common, which opened in 1937 and was purchased by Tottenham Council in the 1960s.

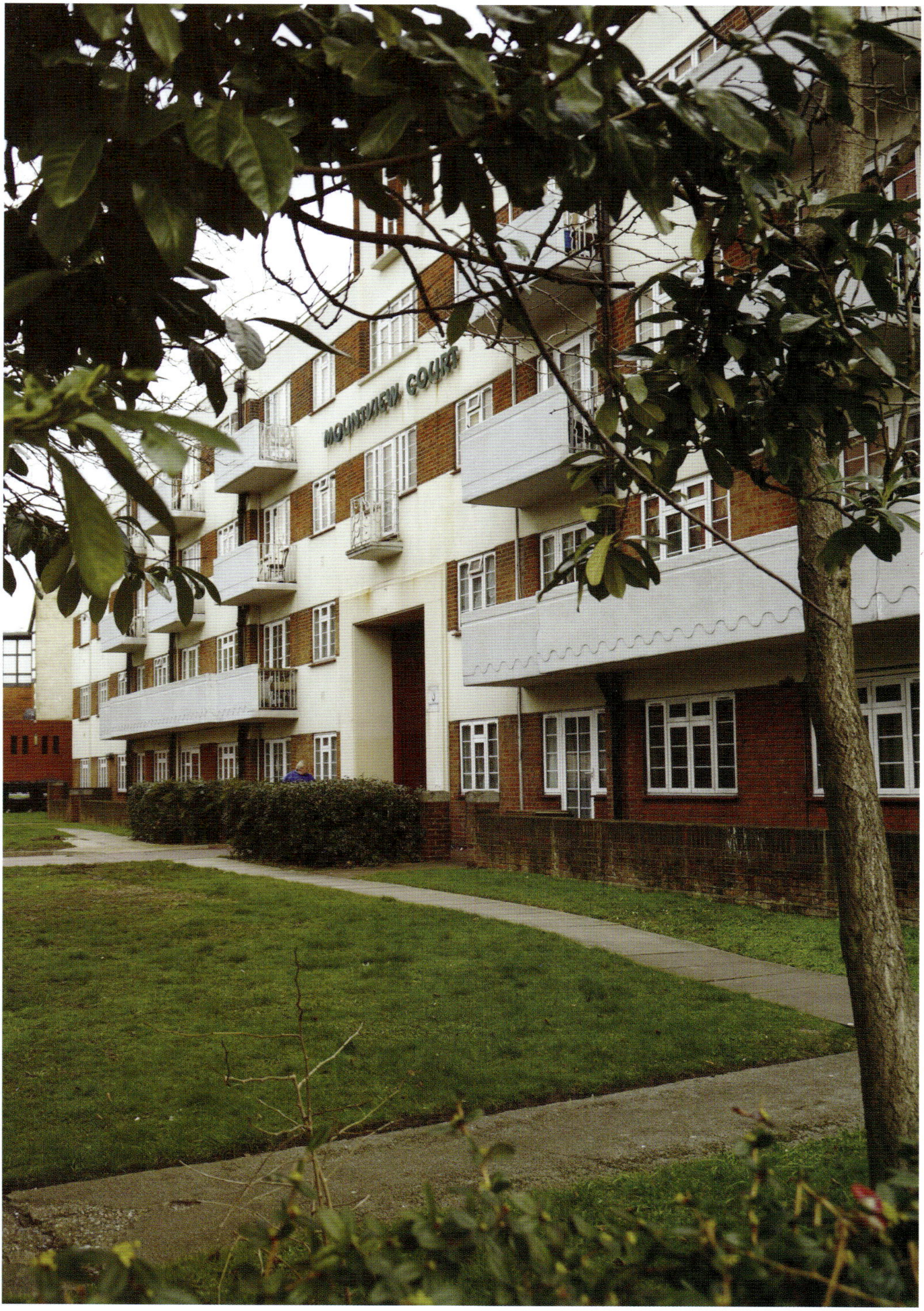
MOUNTVIEW COURT

Salisbury Promenade

Along Green Lanes beyond St Ann's Road [area 1] up to Colina Road, there were no buildings before 1910 when the Coliseum Cinema opened. The cinema closed in 1961 becoming a bingo hall and then a furniture warehouse before it was demolished in 1999.

Behind the Coliseum is the Salisbury Promenade that was built in the 1920s, with shops at ground level, including a Woolworths store beside the Coliseum, and two large rooms above; a billiard hall at the northern end and a fashionable concert/dance hall called the Salon Bal adjoining the cinema. A disastrous fire in 1932 burnt out the Salon Bal slightly damaging the cinema's roof.

Much later on, Woolworth's moved from Salisbury Promenade further along Green Lanes to numbers 17-19 Grand Parade. From the 1930s to 1960 number 17 was Turners' a greengrocers and numbers 18-19 was a costumiers run by Louis Cooper. Woolworths took over the three shops in 1960 and continued there until 1985 when the new shop front was installed for the present day Iceland store, which is out of keeping with the rest of Grand Parade.

Today the cream ceramic tiles of Salisbury Promenade survive and the billiard hall has become a snooker club.

Salisbury Promenade with its cream ceramic tile facing of the 1920s.

SAVOR
TESCO express
24HR CASH
SALISBURY PROMENADE
TESCO express
Collect here
LITTER

Green Lanes Today

Although the shops on Green Lanes have changed since the fine Victorian parades opened in 1900, it remains a vibrant shopping centre. Whereas the shops along Green Lanes in the early 20th century were predominantly small shops selling clothing, food and household items, in the 21st century they are mainly restaurants, fruit and vegetable supermarkets, jewellers, bookmakers and estate agents.

Although many of the shops and their frontages have changed, the superstructure of the buildings has remained much the same as when they were first built. The recent refurbishment of many of the buildings has improved the look of Green Lanes. The Disney store retains the character of the original frontage which opened in 1900 as Hughes Brothers Temple of Fashion in numbers 34-36 Grand Parade. Disney's was first established as a small shop at number 74 Grand Parade in 1913 and only moved to its present position in 1938, taking over from Taylors the house furnishers. In 1953 Mr Disney sold the business to George Smith, but the Disney brothers brought the company back in 1985 and continue to run it today at numbers 34 and 35 Grand Parade.

Originally Harringay was home to the aspiring, mainly English, working class. In the 1970s Harringay became a place of choice for the Cypriot population of north London that was moving away from Camden and Islington. Following the coup in 1974, and the declaration of the Turkish Cypriot state in 1983, Haringey was the borough that absorbed most of the refugees. Today Harringay is a rich mix of English, Cypriot, Turkish, and Eastern European peoples and many of the shops reflect the changes.

Disney's furniture store at 34 and 35 Grand Parade, retaining the appearance of the original Temple of Fashion store.

A Harringay Timeline
(Page Numbers shown in brackets)

1900s	Conway Road Fire Station opened (p10); Salisbury Mansions in St Ann's Road opened (p 44); The Church of St Peter in Wightman Road finally completed (p 10); Williamson Tile & Brick works closed (pp 16, 20 &32); Piccadilly line extension to Finsbury Park (pp 20 &32).
1920s	The Coliseum cinema opened at Salisbury Corner (p 24), The Premier Electric Theatre, facing Duckett's Common, opened (p 28), The Bioscope Picture Palace, junction of Wightman Road and Turnpike Lane, opened (p 28), Hughes Brothers Temple of Fashion, Grand Parade, (p 48), Disney's opens at 74 Grand Parade (p 48), The Boyd piano works opened (p26), Oakwood Laundry, Green Lanes, opened (pp 14 & 24); Hornsey Social Club relocates to Green Lanes (p 36)
1920s	Hornsey and Wood Green affiliated synagogue, Hampden Road, opened (p12); Salisbury Promenade developed (p 46); Harringay Stadium opened (pp 16, 20,32 & 34)
1930s	Piccadilly line extended from Finsbury Park (p 24); Fire burns out Salon Bal, Salisbury Promenade (p 46); The Bioscope Picture House closed (p 28); Harringay Arena opened (p 32); Mountview Court, Green Lanes, opened (p 44), Premier Electric Theatre renamed Regal (p 28).
1940s	War damage (pp 6, 18 & 44); Boyd piano Factory moved from Warwick Gardens (p 26); Ever Ready's central laboratories opened after the war (p 26)
1950s	Mr Disney sells the business to George Smith (p 48); The Regal absorbed by Essoldo (p 28); Harringay Park, Green Lanes, station renamed Harringay Park and then Harringay Stadium (p 42); Home & Colonial Stores Ltd. took over Harringay Arena (p 32).

1960s	Tottenham Council bought Mountview Court (p 44); Woolworths moved from Salisbury Promenade to 17-19 Grand Parade (p 46); The Coliseum cinema closed (p 46); The Regal became a bingo club (p 28); The old goods depot by Harringay Stadium station closed (p 42); Derby Hall Christian Assembly room opened (p 22).
1970s	Re-development of Lords Grove Estate (pp 6, 22 & 30); Hornsey and Wood Green synagogue closed (p12); Harringay Grove redeveloped (p 30); Harringay Arena demolished (p 32).
1980s	Log Cabins Park (p 16); Ever Ready laboratories closed and new flats built by Crabtree (p 26); The St Paul's Church, Wightman Road, burned down (p 12 & 44); New River walking route opened (pp 10, 16 & 40); Railway Fields opened (p 42); Woolworths closed (p 46); Disney's opened again in 34-35 Grand Parade (p 48); Harringay Stadium closed (p 32); Red House care home opened (p 22); The Curzon Cinema closed (p 28).
1990s	The Turkish Youth Association community centre opened (p 36); Harringay Stadium station renamed Harringay East, and then Harringay Green Lanes (p 42); Finsbury Park Avenue developed (p 20); MacDonald's opened (p 32); Sainsbury's opened (p 32);
	New St Paul's Church opened (pp 12 & 44); The Kurdistan Workers' Association took over Fairfax Hall (p 36); New Curzon cinema opened (p 28); Turkish Cypriot Women's project opened Hampden Road (p 36); New Hornsey Mosque built (p 12 & 36), The Coliseum cinema demolished (p 46); Final development of Arena Retail Park and St Anne's Village began (pp 6 & 20).

About the Authors

John Hinshelwood is a local historian who lives on the Harringay Ladder and has a particular interest in the urban development of the ancient parishes that were incorporated into the London Borough of Haringey. After spending seven years as the honorary archivist for the Hornsey Historical Society he studied part time for an MA in Regional and Metropolitan History and has since written several books on the local area, not least How Harringay Happened, published by the Harringay Festival Committee in 2012.

Stephen Rigg is enthusiastically involved in a number of local organisations and met John firstly at the Hornsey Historical Society. At John's instigation, and under his benevolent guidance, he conducted the initial annual Stroud Green Road retail survey – now in its seventh year. He and John surveyed the retail scene in Green Lanes, Hornsey High Street, Crouch End and Muswell Hill Broadway. Since his recent retirement Stephen has undertaken more projects locally and in the City of London.